Yesterday's Wir

No 6
Neston, Parkgate, Heswall
including
Thurstaston, Irby & Greasby

We're feeding well at HESWALL.

Above: Comic Postcard from Heswall

Cover: Middle Slip, Parkgate

ISBN 0-9507255-5-2

Price £6.95

BY THE SAME AUTHORS

Our Village, Neston

Graphic Design: Ian Boumphrey - Desk Top Publisher

Published By: Ian & Marilyn Boumphrey The Nook 7 Acrefield Road Prenton Wirral CH42 8LD
Tel/Fax: 0151 608 7611 e-mail: ian@yesterdayswirral.co.uk
Web Site:www.yesterdayswirral.co.uk
[First published 1999 – reprinted 2003]

Printed By: Bookprint Sl, Barcelona

Introduction

This is the sixth book in our series Yesterday's Wirral in which we once again bring you a selection of photographs which depict Wirral as it used to be. Below is a poem which shows how memories of Wirral remain strong however far away you may be.

Thoughts in Exile

There's bright sunshine here, in Malta; while at home are fog and rain,
With the wet wind in the uplands, and the floods down in the plain.
But, in spite of winter's weather, I would far, far rather be
In the wide, sweet, open country, 'twixt the Mersey and the Dee.

Though the woods are bare and leafless, and the song-birds all are fled;
Though the flowers in the gardens and the hedgerows all are dead;
And the wet west wind comes sweeping in across the Irish sea,
To wake the foam on Mersey Bar and flood the Sands O' Dee;

Yet, spite of wintry storm or rain or fog, I love it all,
And long to be on Thurstaston, as evening's shadows fall;
For no sight is half so beautiful, or half so dear to me,
As the stormy, golden sunsets o'er the gleaming Sands O' Dee.

And when the war is over, with what joy shall I return
To the fields and paths and commons and the woods for which I yearn;
To the moors and the uplands, and the salt kiss of the sea,
In the Hundred of the Wirral, 'twixt the Mersey and the Dee.

This poem was sent to the author of a local publication, The Rambler, by FRANK JOCELYN PRIEST who was away in Malta in 1915 during the First World War.

In 1898 Arthur Kilpin Bulley, a Liverpool cotton broker, built Mickwell Brow, pictured above, on a sandstone outcrop overlooking the River Dee at Ness. His hobby was gardening and he developed part of his large garden as a commercial nursery. This became the seeds and plants firm Bees Limited which moved to a large site at Sealand in 1911. He commissioned travellers abroad to return with plants, many of which were new to this country and were first cultivated at Ness. He was a conservationist who bought Burton Wood and was a member of the group which purchased Thurstaston Hill. These areas were both donated to the National Trust (continued below).

The house pictured above is seen to the right of the willow tree in this 1930 view. The tree collapsed in 1968. Mr Bulley helped the local community by providing recreational facilities and in 1926 he arranged for the families of striking miners to receive provisions from local shops. He died in 1942 and in 1948 his daughter, Lois, presented the gardens together with a £75,000 endowment to Liverpool University. Mrs Bulley continued to live at the house until her death in 1955. Since then the gardens have doubled in size and are open to the paying public all year round.

The old inn pictured here c1890 was the original Royal Oak which stood facing onto the west end of Little Neston Village Green. This thatched building had two unusual chimneys which can be seen on the left. Built in the style of the sixteenth century, they stood out from the building line which left more room inside the inn. William Burkey, the landlord, is probably the man in the shirt sleeves in the centre of those posing for this photograph. Fire destroyed these premises in 1895 and the present Royal Oak was built behind the site of the old one. The large boulder pictured in the foreground was originally found in a field off Badger Bait and is now in Thornton Manor gardens.

Neston Cottage Hospital was originally a private house belonging to William Pritchard. It became a hospital as a memorial to the men of Neston who died in the First World War and is pictured here after 1928 when the single storey extension on the right was built. The Institute at Little Neston which had formerly been in use as a chapel and as a school was demolished to make way for this extension. The hospital buildings were auctioned in 1964 and were then pulled down to make way for residential development. To the left of the hospital is the Little Neston Methodist Church which was built in 1872.

This looks down Bull Hill, Little Neston in 1905. All the cottages on the right are still standing. The farthest one, with its steps leading up to the front door, was once The Bull and Dog Inn which dated back to at least 1850 when it was called The Bull and the victualler was William Roberts. By 1923 it had become a private home. The tall chimney in the background belonged to Hallfield Brickyard which was situated on the corner of Burton Road and Colliery Lane. The latter was so called because it led to Wirral Colliery and is now Marshlands Road. Houses were built on the site of the brickyard after the First World War.

St Winefride Roman Catholic Church is photographed in Burton Road c1913. Originally built as a school in 1840, it was adapted as a chapel in 1843 when the present presbytery was enlarged. The building is a neat Gothic stone structure and was designed by A W N Pugin. Due to an increase in the congregation, further extensions were required in 1852. These included two additional bays each twenty two feet in length and a small gallery for the choir, which together provided one hundred additional seats. The adjacent school and teacher's house built in the Gothic style were added in 1856.

Taken at the crossroads in Chester High Road Hinderton in 1913; Quarry Road off to the left leads to Willaston and Hinderton Road on the right leads to Neston. The centre of this community was the inn which stands at the crossroads and is pictured on the right. It was originally called The Hinderton Arms and has been called The Shrewsbury Arms for at least the last 130 years. In 1860 the victualler was Moses Robertson who was also a veterinary surgeon. Travellers from Chester to Neston would have appreciated stopping here as the roads were then in a dreadful state. The road has since been widened and now includes the gardens seen on the left.

Looking up Hinderton Road away from Neston centre about 1913, the hardware shop on the left, which is now a cobblers, is on the corner of Gladstone Road. Neston Institute which was built as the Liberal Club in 1901/1902 is on the right. It cost £3,000, seated nine hundred people, and included rooms for billiards, smoking and reading, as well as providing baths and lavatories. A verandah running down one side overlooked the bowling green and two tennis courts. During the First World War the building was called Neston Red Cross Hospital and was used to treat wounded soldiers. It is now known as the Civic Hall.

7

Many of the buildings in this 1913 photograph looking up Bridge Street have since been demolished and the road widened. The ones left standing include those in the far background and the Coach and Horses pub which is to the right of the lamp-post and which now incorporates part of the adjoining terraced house as a single storey extension. In 1984 a further extension was built at the back using bricks reclaimed from a derelict barn in the grounds. The dwelling in the right foreground now forms part of the site of Bridge Court which provides sheltered accommodation.

Chester Road is seen from its junction with Bridge Street c1910. The buildings on the right have since been replaced by a block of shops. Some of the terraced cottages on the left are still standing but the white-washed ones were demolished to make way for the Neston New Cinema which opened 18 April 1921 and closed 23 April 1960. It re-opened as the Royal Cinema 13 November 1961 but this closed the following year and became a bingo hall. This venture was short lived and the Neston Royal Shopping Arcade was opened on the site by Ken Dodd 18 November 1984. Neston Institute can be seen in the distance under the bridge.

St Mary and St Helen Church is pictured in High Street, Neston in 1904. This is the second church to be built on the site, the original one dating back to at least the middle of c12. The present tower is partly fourteenth century and the font dates back to at least the sixteenth century. One interesting entry in the Neston registers occurred on 12 May 1765 when Emily Lyon was baptised. The daughter of Henry and Mary Lyon of Ness, she became the famous Lady Hamilton. Due to the poor state of the original building, the church was rebuilt in 1874/5. This Parish Church has two daughter churches, namely St Thomas's, Parkgate and St Michael's, Little Neston.

Pictured in 1918 on the corner of High Street and Brook Street is the old vicarage. This ancient building, which had its own cow-house, piggery and poultry-house, ceased to be a vicarage in 1857. The vicar had a new house built in Wood Lane now called The Woodlands (replaced as a vicarage in 1903 by a house in Parkgate Road, itself replaced in 1985 by a vicarage built next to the parish church). The old vicarage pictured here became a school between 1861 and 1923. The house was then pulled down and Irwin's grocery shop built on the site in 1931. About 1961 Irwin's was taken over by Tesco.

The train is waiting at the platform of Neston & Parkgate Station in Raby Road c1906. This was on the Bidston to Hawarden Bridge Line which opened 18 May 1896. The station was later known as Neston North and when the other Neston station (see below) on the West Kirby to Hooton Line closed in 1962 it became Neston Station. The main use of the line was to convey goods and raw materials to and from Shotton Steel Works. Neston Station is still in use today with two-car passenger diesels plying between Wrexham and Bidston. However, two other stations on the line have closed, Storeton in 1951 and Burton Point in 1955.

This group on the platform of Neston South Station, prior to the First World War, includes the station-master, Mr W Linley, his wife and daughter. This station was on the GWR & LNWR Line which ran from Hooton to West Kirby. The Hooton to Parkgate section of the line opened 1 October 1866 and was extended to West Kirby in 1886. This station closed 15 September 1956 but the line was used for goods until 1962. The station-master's house was occupied until 1970 and later demolished with houses built on the site. The Wirral Country Park now occupies the site of the former Hooton to West Kirby Line.

This horse-drawn delivery cart pictured in 1911 belonged to C L Molyneux who ran a bakery in Park Street, Neston. Loaves of bread can be seen through the window above the advertisement on the side of the vehicle. It was customary at that time for bakers to deliver bread from door to door, much the same as the milkman does today. By 1923 the bakery was owned by William Henry Kinvig. Another business situated in Park Street was The Brewer's Arms which was owned by Birkenhead Brewery and still stands at the junction with High Street. It bears a 1670 date stone.

This group is outside the Wesleyan Chapel in 1917, at the junction of Park Street and High Street. The foundation stone was laid 27 June 1908. The Wesleyan Chapel replaced a non-denominational Mission Hall, an 'iron church'(ie. made of corrugated iron) erected in 1874. This building was bought by Methodists in 1899 and used by them until they erected the present building. Previously, the Methodists had had a chapel in Parkgate Road where John Wesley preached in 1762, but that building was bought by Presbyterians (see page 16) in 1859, and the Methodist presence ceased in Neston for forty years.

Neston Town Hall is pictured in High Street in 1922. Built at a cost of £2,500, it was opened in July 1888. The datestone, together with a crest which includes the three sheaves of Cheshire, can be seen at the top of the centre building. The Neston Picturedrome Company showed films here from 1915 having been forced to move from The Institute when it became a military hospital (see page 7). Films continued to be shown until Neston's first purpose-built cinema opened in 1921 (see page 8). The sign on the left advertises The North & South Wales Bank which later became part of The London Joint City & Midland Bank.

The people posing in front of The Cross (see next picture) include a baby in a penny-farthing perambulator and a young telegraph boy. The building behind them is The White Horse Inn which replaced the original thatched inn after it was demolished in 1877. The inn closed for business in 1960s and offices and a betting shop are now situated there. The nearest building on the right on the corner of Brook Street is The Brown Horse Inn which still stands there today. The Mission Hall in the far distance is mentioned on the previous page.

The drinking fountain at Neston is seen on the right at The Cross c1906 with Parkgate Road off to the centre left. Christopher Bushell, a Liverpool wine merchant and local benefactor, sank a public well on this site which was wheel-pump operated. In recognition of this generosity the local community erected The Bushell Fountain in 1882 which connected with the new water supply which he helped to instigate in his capacity as chairman of the Local Board. Jackson's Tower which is to the left of the fountain was built in 1895 by George Jackson whose chemist shop was next door. The clock-face which is half-way up the tower is no longer there.

The policeman is standing in Parkgate Road which is viewed from the other direction in the previous picture. The old vicarage can be seen in the background (see page 9). Hale's shop on the right advertises high class chocolates and the single-storey building beyond is Billy Beattie's hairdressers.The next building once housed two licensed premises, namely The Black Bull and The Greenland Fishery which were both built in the eighteenth century. Chester Northgate Brewery purchased these adjoining public houses and their application to combine them as The Greenland Fishery was granted in September 1892. The hotel has recently acquired the premises beyond.

13

The ladies are holding flower-topped staffs on this sunny day in 1908, whilst listening to the band, seen on the right. This is the first Thursday in June which is Neston Ladies Day. The two stalwarts on the left are bearing a banner which states, 'Neston Female Friendly Society Established 1814 - Bear ye one another's burdens'. The society members would subscribe regularly to its fund and could then claim financial assistance in times of illness, pregnancy or death. The shops in the background are also pictured below.

This Neston Ladies's Day photograph was taken in 1907. The crowd is lining the route of the procession which is led by a band; then come the two banner bearers who are having trouble controlling the banner in the wind; behind them is a youngster who carries the Lady Patroness's staff which is decorated with flowers; the Lady Patroness with the Mayor and local clergy then follow and behind them are the Society's members. Two vendors in the foreground are selling ribbons and baskets. Nowadays the Ladies of Neston carry the banner for all other female friendly societies, as this is the only one to survive. 14

This photograph was taken looking down Parkgate Road from Neston towards Parkgate in 1913. Vine House pictured on the right was built mid c18. A sun dial is built into the top storey of the front of the house. The most unusual aspect of Vine House is its crinkle crankle wall which forms two sides of its gardens. Dr Russell once lived here and after his death his widow and son donated the land, opposite their house, on which Neston Library was built. The well-known philanthropist, Andrew Carnegie, provided £1,200 towards the building costs. The library, which opened in 1908, can be seen on the left.

Mr Whineray, who was described in 1922 as one of Neston's principal landowners, lived at Leighton Court in Buggen Lane. This road, whose name means ghost, was the southern boundary of Neston Park and is opposite the church pictured at the bottom of the following page. Leighton Court was built in 1889 as a private house for a Liverpool cotton broker, George O'Neill-Bridge, who only lived there for two years. This magnificent building became a casino and country club in the 1960s. A developer purchased the property in the 1980's and, following a fire in 1987, it was demolished. The land still awaits development.

15

The Old Quay House is pictured in a state of dereliction c1918. It was built in c17 and was an inn until about 1710 when it became three dwellings. In 1750 it was leased by the County of Cheshire as the Neston House of Correction, and was used to house Irish vagrants who were being deported to Dublin via Parkgate under the Poor Laws. After 1803 it became a private house until c1915. The building, which had been derelict for some forty years, was reduced to rubble following firing practice by the Home Guard during the Second World War.

Neston Presbyterian Church was founded in 1858 when its first meeting place was a chapel in Parkgate Square. This is now St Thomas's Church of England (see page 23). At the same time they acquired a chapel in Parkgate Road, where John Wesley had preached (see page 11), and also acquired a building in Little Neston (see page 5), using all three together. The present church, which is pictured on the corner of Parkgate Road and Moorside Lane, was built at a cost of £3,000 in 1883/4 and is now called the Parkgate & Neston United Reformed Church. The manse which is pictured on the right was erected in 1900.

16

This hay-making scene was photographed c1910. The new house on the right was the first to be built in Earle Drive. The left hand part, Parkside, is now an Abbeyfield Home with the right side, Woodhill House, standing at the junction with Wood Lane. Two ladies on the left are walking down the tree-lined Earle Drive, which was built in 1903 between Parkgate Road and Leighton Road. "Leighton Park Estate" was a name invented by the developer (N A Earle) and no "Leighton Park" ever existed. The land here was once part of Neston Park, a medieval deer park. This picture was taken from what is now Woodlands Road, where development took place during the 1960s.

Leighton Road is seen in 1913, looking towards Neston. Leighton Croft which was built c1840 is on the left opposite Neston mill. Originally there were two mills but one was demolished after being severely damaged by a storm in 1822. The remaining mill was last used in the 1880's. In 1975, Robert Ellison and Lesley Blackburne purchased the mill and it had a new lease of life as The Old Mill Gallery. It was from here that they operated a glass engraving business which ceased in 1990 when Bob Ellison retired.

17

The 1st Worcester Artillery Volunteers are marching from Parkgate Station, in the background, to set up camp in the Park Fields on 5 August 1906. This was a popular venue for military camps and were usually artillery as they were able to fire guns onto the estuary. Parkgate Station was opened in 1866 on the Hooton to Parkgate Line. When this line was extended to West Kirby in 1886 the station was moved from the original site on the south (Neston) side of Station Road to the north (Parkgate) side. The line was closed to passengers in 1956 and to goods in 1962. In 1969 it became part of the Wirral Country Park.

Cheshire Automobile Club arranged for Henri Salmet, the French aviator, who was on a publicity tour with the Daily Mail, to give an aviation display at Leighton Park, Parkgate on 8 July 1914. The crowd looks on eagerly as Salmet's Bleriot-Gnome monoplane moves forward in front of the specially erected marquee hangar ready for take-off. A previous aviation visit to Parkgate took place two years earlier on 16 July 1912 when Mr King of Freshfield flew along the Wirral coast from New Brighton via Hoylake and Heswall. He landed his Farman biplane on Parkgate shore at 8.30pm.

18

Neston Cricket Club is pictured at its Parkgate ground in 1913. The club was founded in 1894 by Dr Henry Speechly, who was its first captain. The initial game was played on this ground in 1895, which was leased until the club purchased the main ground in 1922 and in 1977 the rear field was bought from Mostyn House School. Following a fire which destroyed the clubhouse in 1971, the present clubhouse was built. Besides cricket, the club's sports are squash and tennis and it boasts one of the country's top hockey sections. Indoor sports including snooker and table tennis as well as bridge, are played.

The building seen in the foreground in 1917, is the Old Custom House which was on the south side of Station Road. Due to the movement of the main River Dee channel from the English to the Welsh side of the estuary, Parkgate's importance as a port died out. The Custom House was no longer used by 1821, and the last Customs Officer left Parkgate in 1828. In the early 1960s The Old Custom House, which had by then become The Cosy Cafe, was demolished along with all the other buildings pictured here. The Old Quay Pub which opened in 1963 was built on this site by Birkenhead Brewery and part of Parkgate's heritage had gone for ever.

Mostyn House School incorporates the single storey buildings on the right and the two adjoining ones in this 1890s scene. The buildings include The George Inn which was first recorded in 1779. This became The Mostyn Arms Hotel in 1819 which was successfully run by Esther Briscoe until her death in 1855. It was then purchased by Edward Price who moved his school here from Tarvin and gave it its present name. From 1862 the school was run by his wife's nephew, Rev A S Grenfell, whose son became headmaster in 1890. The school thrived for many years as a preparatory school. Pupils may now attend until the age of sixteen and girls have been admitted since 1976.

It is hard to imagine that there was once sand at Parkgate but this 1913 photograph shows that this was so. It was a fashionable bathing place in the mid eighteenth century and early nineteenth century but then declined. Lady Hamilton, who became Lord Nelson's mistress and had been born at Ness, returned here to be treated for a skin complaint by bathing in the sea. She reputedly stayed at Dover Cottage which is the end house in Station Road opposite the present Old Quay Inn. Mostyn House School, which is marked by a cross, has been extended since the previous picture. Its present black and white frontage dates from 1932.

The first building on the right c1900 has a dark sign on the side wall advertising 'Acton's Union Family Hotel'. There had been several buildings on this site including the Post Office, a school, two inns and several private houses. In 1862 The Union Hotel which incorporated most of these was opened. It was over a century later that the name of the hotel was changed to The Ship, the name of one of the former inns sited here. Hilbre House adjoining The Union was demolished in the 1960s and a single-storey extension to The Ship Hotel is now sited here. Beyond that is Dee House which was replaced by a block of shops in 1935 where Nicholl's famous ice cream is still sold.

This 1937 photograph shows part of the promenade which is known as The Donkey Stand jutting out seawards. Towards the end of the last century children could take rides on donkeys from here as far as South Slip and back for 2d. Originally a tall, narrow building had stood on this site. It became Parkgate's first Assembly House in the 1780s. In 1812 the house was converted into sea-water baths for the convenience of invalids who were unable to plunge into the sea. The building had been demolished by 1840 and the people on the benches are enjoying uninterrupted views of the River Dee and the Welsh hills.

This high-tide photographed in 1938 is seen washing the walls of The Red Lion. When the tide was this high, residents and visitors would use Cheltenham Walk which is now called Rope Walk. This goes from Station Road. to Coastguard Lane which comes out in Mostyn Square and a wiend called Little Lane goes off it which enters The Parade by Nicholl's shop. The Red Lion dates back to at least 1822 and was run by the Wood family for most of the nineteenth century. One feature of this pub, which is the oldest surviving Parkgate inn to have remained relatively unchanged, is the hanging sign advertising 'Walker's Warrington'.

The tide has gone out leaving small pools and two stranded boats in this 1930s photograph. Alma Cottage which takes its name from a battle in the Crimean War is the dark building on the right and was built in 1855. The central building is Holywell House.It was erected as a pair of villas, replacing a large house, and was converted into a single dwelling in 1918. It was run as the Holywell Hotel for thirty years and in 1956 became the first residential home for elderly diabetics in the north of England. It is now The Parkgate Nursing Home. The building on the left is The Warren which was rebuilt in 1906.

The Parkgate fisherman on the left was known as Six Foot Smith, because of his lack of height! The men are mending their nets in Mostyn Square in 1918. Behind them is St Thomas's Church which was built in 1843 by the Congregationalists who had previously worshipped in The Assembly Rooms on The Parade. It was taken over by the Presbyterians in 1858, prior to their move to Neston (see page 16). The Parkgate chapel was not used again until leased by The Church of England in 1910. They purchased the building seven years later and named it St Thomas's - The Fisherman's Church.

The first door on the right is the entrance to Platts Cottage from where Colin Mealor, Parkgate's last fisherman, now operates. It was from a table in the doorway of the adjoining house, Hill View, that his father started Parkgate's first shrimp shop. The fishing grounds were then off Hilbre Island and Point of Ayr and are the same today, but his fishing boat is now moored at Thurstaston. The shop next door which is now called Parkgate Stores was run for many years by the Howe family. The adjoining building which is currently a Chinese restaurant was once Prosser's General Stores.

This is a 1930s scene outside Leeman's Garage on The Parade at Parkgate. The business, which was originally in Station Road, moved here in the 1920s and was AA listed from 1918 until 1957. The breakdown vehicle pictured has been converted from a car and is towing a van belonging to Strawson's of Liverpool. Regent Oil purchased the property in 1957 and the garage was run firstly by Gerrard Motors and later by Bowmans. The convalescent home next door (pictured below) was demolished in the 1950s when this area became part of the garage car park. In the mid 1980s the garage site was sold and warden assisted flats were built here.

Parkgate Convalescent Home which opened in 1882 was situated in this building. This 1915 photograph shows the unusual square facade which was built to shore up the building which was leaning towards the river front. During the First World War it was used as a Red Cross hospital and was demolished in the 1950s (see above). The building in the background was originally a single residence dating from the early eighteenth century. It now forms two houses, Overdee to the left and Greywalls on the right.

24

This 1915 photograph was taken by George Davies, a photographer from New Ferry. The horses are being led by Lieutenant Mike Rimington who ran a horse reformatory and riding school from stables in Station Road. An advertising postcard of his states, 'Mankillers Converted'. He has just passed a building called Moaney Moar which is now The Moorings. This is one of only two houses on The Parade which now has a gable end facing the river. In the distance is a car which would be a fairly unusual sight for this period.

The Parkgate fishermen are shown unloading their haul of shrimps, cockles and mussels onto horse drawn carts on The Middle Slip c1930. The majority of their catch would be taken either to Parkgate Station from where the trains would carry them to the larger towns and cities of the northwest, or to Birkenhead and then by ferry to Liverpool and beyond. The remainder of the catch would be sold locally by the fishermen who were then thirty in number. Now only one survives (see page 23). There are two other slipways at either end of the promenade.

Parkgate.

The Watch House, the building pictured on the left c1916, is seen jutting out into the road by The Middle Slip just as it does today. From 1799 to 1828 the Customs leased this property as an observation post for the use of their men whose own building was not well-placed for a look-out (see page 19). They had to keep an eye on the dangerous shifting channels and on any attempted smuggling. Illicit goods confiscated by the customs officers could be purchased at the regular sales held at The Custom House. These goods included brandy, rum, starch, hair powder, soap, cotton, linen, vinegar and salt.

The photographer was standing on The Middle Slip when he took this picture. The Watch House, pictured above, is seen on the left. It was here in 1884 that John Pride, a local artist and poet, stayed at the age of seven. He was excited to wake up to find that the house had been cut off on three sides by the rising tide. In the 1930s at least seven of his Parkgate sketches, three accompanied by poems, were published as postcards. The building beyond, which is now called The Moorings, was once called Moaney Moar (Manx for moor house). The old abandoned boats were landmarks on the slipway for many years.

The caption on this postcard, which is dated 1906, states Ryley's Castle, Parkgate. This refers to the white-washed cottage on the extreme left which was once owned by Samuel Ryley, an actor and strolling player who organised a theatre company in Parkgate c1815. He was a jovial character, perpetually in debt who loved Parkgate and referred to his dwelling as a cottage of content. Part of the old cottage was supposedly incorporated into The White House, which was built on this site in the 1920s.

The Sawyer's Arms pictured centre c1906 has lighter stonework above the door where a sign-board once bore its name. This tiny alehouse's first landlord was probably Richard Bartley, a carpenter and sawyer, who held an aleseller's licence in 1793. The first record of its name (as with many pubs) was in 1822. One source gives the inn as the Carpenter's Arms. The inn closed in 1905. The building to the right is called Pengwern after the Pengwern Arms (this was named after one of the seats of the Mostyn family who owned the whole village until 1849), which once stood on the site of The Boathouse (page 29). Dee Cottages are to the left.

This view of a stormy day at Parkgate was taken in the early 1930s when the tide regularly came up to the sea wall. The black and white half-timbered building in the left background is The Boathouse Cafe (see opposite page). The next row of buildings is Dee Cottages and Brooke House is on the right. A sandy area was still here at the end of the Second World War. By this time the Dee was silting up fast, the local fishermen were operating off Heswall, and spartina grass was taking a hold by the South Slip. Today the tide comes up to the wall about a dozen times a year.

This aerial view of the north end of Parkgate was taken c1930. The Boathouse Cafe (see opposite page) is silhouetted against the River Dee in the background. Part of Boathouse Lane can be seen through the trees on the right which shelter the large house, Leighton, from the road. Joseph Rich had this house built in 1862, and called it Richville. He was declared bankrupt within three years! At the turn of the century it was known as Leighton and between the two World Wars it was used by Miss May Richardson as a girls' school. About 1950 it became a hotel and is now called The Parkgate Hotel.

28

The Boat House Cafe, Parkgate.

The Boathouse Cafe is pictured here in 1928 two years after it was built. An aerial view would have shown that the outline was in the form of a boat. It was erected on the site of an old coaching inn, The Pengwern Arms, whose outbuildings can be seen in the centre of the picture below. It was from here that the first regular ferry service between Parkgate and Flint operated c1740. This continued until 1864. The ferry service was connected to Birkenhead, Hooton and Chester by a horse-drawn coach service. Following storm damage, The Pengwern Arms was demolished in 1885. The present building is now a restaurant.

The swimmers and sunbathers are enjoying themselves at Parkgate Baths in the early 1930s. Built in 1923 by Mr A G Grenfell, headmaster of Mostyn House School, the open-air pool was intended primarily for the use of his pupils but was also opened to the paying public. Although a children's pool was added in 1930, the baths' long-term use must have been in doubt since they relied on water from the Dee to fill the pools. As the water-level fell in the river, the prohibitive cost of piping water in meant the closure of the baths after the end of World War Two. The site is now a car park for Wirral Country Park.

The Farmers Arms Inn is pictured on Chester High Road at Leighton c1910. It stood on a site opposite Boathouse Lane and served as a wayside inn for travellers on the road from Hoylake to Chester. The licensing laws in Leighton at that time differed from those which applied in Gayton and Heswall where closing time was half an hour earlier. It is said men drank their last pint in The Glegg Arms at Gayton and then proceeded to The Farmers Arms to consume their final drink. The publican prior to 1912 was George Price. By 1922 the premises had ceased to be used as a pub and was run as refreshment rooms (see below).

This 1920s photograph looks along Chester High Road with a side-on view of the refreshment rooms which were formerly The Farmers Arms pictured above. The entrance to the left of the nearest telegraph pole is to the garage which belonged to E G Davis & Company. This garage, later to become Leighton Motors, was ideally situated and now covers an area extending beyond and incorporating the old inn. The building in the distance is Bridges House Farm which still stands today. The road has since been straightened and is now dual carriageway.

The white-washed cottage is described on this 1917 postcard as 'The Old Turnpike Cottage, Gayton'. It was also known as Toll Bar Cottage and was built on the main route from Chester to Hoylake, opposite Gayton Lane. The publisher of this and several other postcards in this book, in the E R J's Wirral series, is Mr E R Jones who is standing on the right next to his trap and pony Dolly. The cottage was last occupied in 1965 and planning permission to extend it was refused in 1981. Following vandalism, a windowless building was erected here.

This hostelry which was built c1840 was once named Crabbe's Inn after Edward Crabbe who was the landlord in the 1850s and 1860s. His son, George, replaced him and ran the inn until c1890. The sign on this 1892 photograph shows that the publican is J Brownlie and that the premises are now called Glegg's Arms, taking their name from the Glegg family who owned Gayton Estate from 1330 to 1921. A public weigh bridge is in front of the single-storey building in the background. A verandah was built in front of the inn c1904 which provided shelter for penny-in-the-slot machines. The inn is now a Beefeater Hotel.

31

Heswall Mill.

Gayton Mill which overlooks Telegraph Road near the corner of Mill Lane was in a state of dereliction when this photograph was taken c1904. It was the oldest tower mill in Wirral, was built of sandstone and bears the date 1735. It was last worked c1860. The then miller's wife bore sixteen children who were raised in the small miller's cottage nearby. Over the years there has been much talk of restoring this listed building. Planning permission was eventually granted for a small housing development which was to blend in with the mill and restoration work finally commenced in 1990.

The clubhouse of Heswall Golf Club is pictured in 1904. Founded in 1902, the club used part of Leighton Hall Farm as its clubhouse until the one pictured here was ready. This was burnt down 20 January 1924 when the two-storey building constructed entirely from pitch pine was found alight by a boy who informed the licensee of The Hotel Victoria. He called out Birkenhead Fire Brigade and it was able to save the bungalow and farm buildings adjoining the clubhouse. Estimated damage was put at £10,000. Two army huts provided temporary accommodation until the new clubhouse opened in June 1926.

The train is waiting on the West Kirby bound platform of Heswall Station c1905. This section of the line from Parkgate to West Kirby was opened 19 April 1886. The line closed to passengers 17 September 1956 and to goods 7 May 1962. An eight acre site adjoining and forming part of the line was sold for £30,250 in 1966. Houses were erected on this land which fronts onto Davenport Road and Riverbank Road with Riverbank Close now occupying the station site. This was the only part of the railway to be sold off before work on the Wirral Way started in 1969. This opened in 1973. The cottages on the extreme left still survive (see picture below).

Looking up Riverbank Road c1930, the building in the background which faces down the road is the cottages seen on the left in the picture above. These cottages sill stand today in what is now Riverbank Close. All the other buildings pictured above have gone, including the railway cottages which are to the right in both photographs. The only other building at Heswall Station which survives today is the station-master's house, close to which the photographer of the above scene would have stood. The houses on the left which date from 1896 are still standing.

These Heswall shrimpers are posing with their catch down by the River Dee in 1918. The cart on the right holds three full containers of shrimps and a further two are held by the men to its left. At this time there were two fishermen listed in Heswall, Richard Evans and John Lewis, whose families both lived in Station Cottages (see page 33). Previous generations of the Evans family had lived in Parkgate but moved to Heswall as the Dee began to silt up. The houses in the right background stand at the bottom of Park West.

Tiger Smith is seen by the doorway to his thatched cottage in Gayton Road. Beyond Station Road on the left is Stivelooms which is said to date from the seventeenth century. This building, whose front door originally faced onto the road, was extended and rendered at the turn of this century. Behind the overhanging trees and sandstone wall on the right is Roscote. This was the country home of Thomas Brocklebank, which was built in the 1860s and demolished in the 1960s. Wallrake is off to the right and the building this side, formerly an inn called The White Lion, which closed in 1902, is now White Lodge.

This group of postmen and post boys poses by the steps leading to Heswall Post Office c1905. This single-storey building on the left dated 1899 can be seen in the photograph below. Previously the Post Office had been situated in Smallwoods Bakery & General Store which adjoined the ivy-clad house on the right. It moved here because the authorities would not allow the Post Office to operate from the same premises as the bakery which the postmaster, Mr Smallwood, also owned. The workman on the left has string tied round both trouser legs. This was a ploy used by manual workers to prevent vermin running up their legs.

The Post Office building pictured above is seen here in 1930. By this time the Post Office had moved to what was the ivy-clad house on the right, the former Post Office had become a shop and Smallwood's bakery off to the right had become a branch of Lloyd's Bank. The two shops in the centre which were built in the mid 1920s are Brierley's on the right, which dealt in tobacco and stationery, and L E Drew's who was a greengrocer and florist. Barney Mosley is standing on the left talking to Billy Byrne who is riding his motorbike and side-car which advertises his fishmonger's business.

Heswall Parish Church of St Peter is pictured on this 1906 postcard. The first church on this site dated back to c1300 and survived until 1737 when the minister, Rev John Norris, set about replacing most of the old structure. The new church was completed in 1739 and only the tower remained from the old one. This part of the building gave cause for concern and in 1847 records show that work was carried out on the tower by local craftsmen. These included a stonemason, William Boumphrey, (a relative of the author) to whom payment of £19 was made. Following the great storm of 1875 when much structural damage occurred, the present church save the tower was rebuilt.

The Heswall Hotel is shown c1910 at the junction of School Hill and The Village. Built in 1872, it was originally named The Black Horse but when Mr Leeman was the licensee, from 1898 to 1910, it was called The Heswall Hotel. At that time it was residential, having thirteen bedrooms, a public dining room and billiards room. Mrs Leeman prepared speciality ham and egg teas for Sunday ramblers and cyclists which cost 1/6d (7.5p). The maid seen in the window above the entrance would then have received a weekly wage of 3/6d (17.5p). The hotel officially reverted to its former name, The Black Horse, in 1940.

Elder Cottage and Black Horse Hotel, Heswall   No. BH1

The thatched sandstone building on the left with steps leading up to the front door is Elder Cottage which dates from 1686. This was the original school house and in 1847 there were sixty pupils on the school roll. The school extended into the cottage on the left which dates from 1840. This later became the local library. In 1872 the school moved to new purpose-built premises in School Hill (see picture below). Elder Cottage was demolished in 1954 and this narrow section of the road was widened. In 1955 the cottage housing the library was restored in memory of Geoffrey R Mellor. It is now a children's church.

In 1872 Heswall-cum-Oldfield Church School moved from its previous premises, seen above, to the buildings pictured here in 1918. Following the damage caused by the great storm of 1875, church services were held here during the rebuilding of St Peter's. The school was enlarged several times to accommodate the population increase. In 1941 the school received a direct hit from a German bomb which destroyed the headmaster's house and part of the other buildings. In May 1961 St Peter's Church of England School opened in Thurstaston Road (see next page), replacing these premises which became Richmond Hall.

37

St Peter's Church of England Primary School is in the centre of this mid 1960s photograph with its playground to the front and its playing fields to the right. Its previous premises (see last picture) can be seen on School Hill, to the top right of the football pitches. Such was the impact of school when it opened 19 May 1961 that several small private schools in the Heswall area saw a decline in their numbers and decided to close. The school is situated in Thurstaston Road which runs from the bottom right of this aerial view past the school and widens before sweeping right into Dee View which continues almost to the top right.

Looking down Dee View Road in 1911, the board above the bicycle on the right tells us that the licensee of The Dee View Inn is John Fisher and that he sells Allsopp's ales and stout. The building to the right of the dog is a branch of the wine merchants Mackie & Gladstone whose lease expired in 1914. All the buildings adjacent to the inn were demolished and the site is now the pub car park. Pupils from the school (see page 37) are standing by the newsagents and the building beyond is Branch Eleven of the Birkenhead Co-operative Society. At present this is an antique shop.

Heswall Castle, known as Tytherington's Folly, was built about 1870 on a site at the corner of The Mount and Telegraph Road. By the time this photograph was taken in 1902 this castellated building had become a country home for a female orphan asylum. In the background to the right of The Castle are two of three pairs of semis which stood on the far side of Telegraph Road. One of these houses today forms part of Lingham's Bookshop. Plans to convert the folly into council offices in 1934 were not accepted and it was demolished the following year. In 1936 Castle Buildings were erected on part of the site.

John Irwin, Sons & Company opened a grocery store in Pensby Road in 1923. This photograph taken in 1930 shows the staff standing outside. Included is Jack Seaton, the tall van driver on the left, and amongst those in white overalls second from left is Ernest Coupland, who was the manager. Third from left is Ronnie Lightfoot and behind the two men on the extreme right is Beattie Davies who worked here from 1923 until 1959. Liverpool based Irwin's had more than two hundred branches when taken over by Tesco Stores c1960. The Heswall premises were later enlarged and modernised.

This photograph was taken in Telegraph Road at its junction with Pensby Road to the left and The Mount on the right c1911. Lloyd's Bank, the sandstone building to the right, dates from c1904. In 1990 it was proposed to demolish this fine-looking building as it created a bottle-neck at the junction but permission was refused. The trees and wall beyond the bank had been removed some time previously and the building line set further back. To the left of the group with the bicycle is a fenced-off area between the shops where work on the building of King's Hall has just started (see below).

King's Hall is the central part of these premises which were built by John Pye in Telegraph Road in 1912. Films were first shown here in 1916 but it was not until 1928 that the modernised King's Cinema opened on the ground floor with the hall upstairs being used for ballroom dancing etc. Heswall Hill (Heswall-on-the-Hill, not Heswall Hills) Post Office operated from the shop on the left from 1912 until 1919 when it moved to Pensby Road. In 1958 the entire building was offered for sale. The purchaser was Lennons and it became a supermarket. Today two separate shops occupy the building.

This 1908 photograph shows reflections on the Puddydale. This four acre site was given to the local parish by the Enclosure Commissioners c1855. The pond which occupied the Telegraph Road end of the Puddydale was very popular for sailing model boats and for ice skating when the weather permitted. The pool was filled in by the council around the time of the First World War and the land levelled and grassed. In 1909 the Council School opened which was built on land to the right of this picture overlooking the Puddydale. This school closed in 1982 and the buildings were demolished. Flats now occupy the site.

The nine acre site for the Royal Liverpool Children's Hospital was purchased for £2,500 in 1900. It was situated on land bordering onto Telegraph Road, opposite the Puddydale pictured above. The foundation stone was laid 21 April 1905 and following fund-raising events, the first patients were admitted in February 1909. The clock tower pictured centre was opened in 1911. The planned closure of the hospital by the Mersey Regional Health Authority in 1981 was delayed by local pressure for four years and was finally implemented in 1985. The building was demolished during 1989 and in 1991 a supermarket is planned for the site.

The photographer stood in Telegraph Road c1910 to take this picture. Telegraph Road continues into Heswall to the left beyond the two horse-drawn carts. Thurstaston Road which is off to the right was once the more important route when Heswall (now known as Lower Heswall) was the main village and Heswall-on-the-Hill (known as Heswall today) consisted of only a few houses. The triangular piece of land between the two roads is still an open space. This is due to some local residents who purchased the land and gave it to the council in order to prevent a brewery from buying the plot and building a pub on the site.

This aerial view of Cleaver Hospital was taken c1951 with Oldfield Road running behind it. Opened in 1902, the hospital was originally called The West Derby, Liverpool and Toxteth Joint Hospital. By about 1920 it was known as Cleaver Sanatorium, after Mr H P Cleaver, the inspiration behind its founding. By 1913 it had become a children's hospital and in 1939, after the youngsters evacuation to Rhuddlan, adult patients moved in. From 1950 its name was changed to Cleaver Hospital and in 1988 the site was sold for housing development for an estimated £2.5million.

Pensby Road, Pensby is seen in this 1930s picture with Rosemead Avenue off to the left of the shops which were built in 1930. The second shop from the left which has advertising placards and a post box outside is the Post Office which was originally housed in premises on the other side of the road in what is now The 8 O'Clock Shop. The land beyond the farthest parked car is where the library now stands. In 1921 the population of Pensby was 197 and it rapidly increased to 3,000 by 1951 and to 7,500 in 1981. In the far distance the Pensby Hotel can be seen.

Two girls are posing in Pensby at the entrance to A E Jones's General Stores at the junction of Pensby Road and Gills Lane. There are no buildings to be seen to the right of the children on the far side of Pensby Road in this 1918 photograph. At the turn of the century when the local population numbered forty eight Pensby Road was called Pensby Lane and the owner of the shop was W J Anderson. The blank window above the entrance then advertised, 'Cyclist Rest - Refreshments - Good Stabling', and teas were served in a room to the left which fronted onto Gills Lane.

St Bartholomew's Church, Thurstaston, is pictured here c1934. The first mention of a church at Thurstaston was made in 1125 and that building survived until 1820 when it was demolished. The church that replaced it in 1824 was a plain stone edifice which stood for some sixty-one years. The main body of the church was demolished in 1885, but the tower survived and is seen to the left of the church in this photograph and is also pictured below to the left of Thurstaston Hall. The present church, shown here, was consecrated in 1886. It was built in memory of Joseph Hegan by his daughters and cost £6,000.

The history of Thurstaston Old Hall can be traced back to 1070 when Hugh Lupus presented the manor to his relative Robert de Rodelent. There is a possibility that a building then existed on the site of the present hall. The oldest portion is the west wing which dates back to c1350 and can be seen on the right of this 1920s photograph. The central portion, with its curious roof screen with dummy oval windows, was built c1680 and the east wing was added in 1835. An unusual fact is that the hall, which is said to be haunted, has never been offered for sale as it has been passed down from generation to generation.

Dawpool School is pictured in Station Road, Thurstaston. Built in 1858 by Joseph Hegan, the then owner of the Dawpool Estate, it was described as a handsome stone building where, in 1860, some seventy children were taught by M A Jeffrey. In 1902 the school became known as Dawpool National School. This building ceased to be used when the school moved to new premises which were opened in School Lane on 27 January 1906 (see page 48). It was then purchased for £100 by Mrs Margaret Ismay who had been instrumental in the building of the new school. The old school is now a private residence.

The original Dawpool House was built by James Hegan in 1865. Thomas Ismay purchased the 390 acre estate in 1877 and had the house demolished. The foundation stone for a new residence was laid in 1882. Built of red sandstone taken from Heswall Hill Quarry, it was opened in 1884 and is pictured here c1910. In 1917 the then owner, Mr F W P Rutter, loaned Dawpool for use as an officers' orthopaedic hospital. A garden party in aid of Hoylake & West Kirby Cottage Hospital on 18 September 1926 was the last function to be held here. In 1927, after the sale of all interior and exterior fittings, the house was demolished.

This postcard of Thurstaston Station was posted in 1911. The station was opened in 1886 when the GWR & LNWR Line from Hooton to Parkgate was extended to West Kirby. Originally the line was to have been built further inland, closer to Thurstaston village. However, since Thomas Ismay who was the chairman of the railway company did not want the railway to operate so close to his home, Dawpool (see previous picture), it was re-routed. The line was closed to passengers in 1956 and to goods in 1962. It now forms part of the Wirral Way. The Wirral Country Park visitor's centre is off to the left, and Thurstaston village to the right.

The station master, Bill Doig, is seen surveying the damage caused by a head-on collision at Thurstaston Station on Monday 25 February 1957. As mentioned above the station had closed to passenger trains in 1956 but remained open for freight. The train from West Kirby, pictured left, struck the ex-LMS Jinty 0-6-0 engine head-on at 6.15am. Both trains and four wagons were derailed. The freight train driver and his mate escaped harm but their guard, the other driver and fireman suffered minor injuries.This is the only recorded collision on the line. The railway cottages on the left have been demolished.

Thurstaston Camp, pictured in the 1930s, was owned and run by Lever Brothers for their employees use. Sited on the river side of the railway line overlooking the Welsh coast, the land was acquired in 1919. The camp opened in 1921 and comprised army huts which accommodated ninety in the men's section and sixty in the ladies' and later family accommodation was made available. Activities included tennis, cricket, football, and dancing. The camp closed at the outbreak of war in 1939 and was then used by an anti-aircraft battery as part of Liverpool's defences.

Shore Cottages at Thurstaston were aptly named, as they stood just above the shoreline at the foot of rugged boulder clay cliffs. Described as the loneliest cottages in Wirral, one of them was lived in by Sally McCrae and is still known locally as Sally's Cottage even though she died in 1953. Between the wars Sally had teas and refreshments on sale to her many visitors. She also ran a shop from the porch of her home. More recently the cottages have been renovated and transformed into one six- bedroomed detached residence. The dwelling is still as inaccessible and isolated as ever, but that is probably one of its attractions.

47

This 1930s photograph is taken from Thurstaston Common. Camping was popular then and tents can be seen in the centre and far right of the picture. Beyond the tents, houses are under construction. Dawpool National School is on the left. It was built by Margaret Ismay in memory of her husband, Thomas, the founder of the White Star Line, who died in 1899. The foundation stone was laid in 1905 and the school opened on 27 January 1906 on the north-east edge of the common. In 1951 a new primary school was opened in Coombe Road, Irby. This relieved the pressure on Dawpool School.

Taken in 1906, this rural scene is of Thurstaston Road, Irby when it was little more than a cart track. Thurstaston Hill is on the horizon to the left and beneath it is Dawpool School (see picture above). To the right of the road in the distance, is Laburnam Cottage which dates back to at least 1830, when it was shown on Bryant's map of Cheshire. Across the road is Rose Cottage which was run as Irby Tea Gardens by Miss Owen. The three buildings mentioned are still standing today, although the scene is somewhat different. Between the wars, houses were built on both sides of the road.

The rear part of the Anchor Inn was once a seventeenth century cottage. This became Irby's only fully licensed public house. (The Prince of Wales was built in the latter half of the nineteenth century and was licensed for beer only - see page 53). The front of the Anchor was built by Mr Thomas Rowland in the late nineteenth century. It was his nephew, Mr Rowland Cross, who sold the inn for £12,000 at auction in June 1940 to Birkenhead Brewery. The inn had been in the Rowland family for some fifty years. The outbuildings in the background have been demolished and the car park now occupies the site.

Irby Hall is built on the site of the ancient manor house of Saint Werburgh's Abbey, Chester. It was also the home of the Glegg family who founded Calday Grange Grammar School in 1636. The present hall was built in the early seventeenth century and is photographed here when it was still all half-timbered prior to its re-construction in 1888. In 1911 John Ravenshaw leased the farm from the Glegg Estate. The 160 acres covered most of the land between Irby Road and Thurstaston Road up to the present Pensby School. The Hall was sold in 1969 and restored 1970.

Taken from the grounds of Irby Hall (see previous picture), this photograph looks across Irby Road and into Thingwall Road in 1917. The building on the right behind the tree is Corner House Farm which was demolished in the 1930s when the road was widened as a result of the increase in motor traffic. Broster's yard now stands behind the site of the farm. Manor Farm, dating back to c1640, together with its outbuildings, can be seen on the left. This small stone house with its mullioned and hooded windows, was described as a 'little gem' by F C Beazley in his book, Thurstaston, published in 1924 (see picture below).

Manor Farm (see picture above) is shown on the left in Thingwall Road, Irby c1930. The farm buildings were condemned in 1960, but following strong representations from the Wirral Society and other bodies, the order was withdrawn in 1962. By 1967, having been derelict for some years, and suffered from vandalism and weather-damage, the buildings were demolished. The site of the once picturesque farm house is now occupied by the library and public conveniences. The first shop, to the left of the tree, is The Willow Cafe and Tea Gardens which is now the Oak Tub store.

Rookery Farm is pictured in Thingwall Road c1916. That year the farm was purchased by Mr Arthur Constantine. Mr Jones was the tenant farmer until the early 1920s when a private school was opened here. The Irby Literary Society met weekly during 1928 and 1929. In the early 1930s the premises became vacant and, following an idea suggested by Frank Dodd and Joe Roberts, Irby & District Social Club took them over. With help from Yates Brewery, the building was altered and adapted, opening to members in 1933. The farm outbuildings were demolished and Irby Mission, together with the block of shops which now contains Barclay's Bank, were built on the site.

This north side view of Irby Farm was taken from Thingwall Road in 1904. The building was formerly the residence of the Ball family and the datestone on the north gable includes the initials W B and E B 1613, standing for William and Ellen Ball. There is also a 1731 datestone over the east door. The pond which is shown on the right now forms part of the grassed garden. A veterinary surgeon's practice now operates from the old farm house.

This photograph taken in Thingwall Road in 1904, shows the only shop in the village at that time. This was also the Post Office and was run by Mrs Leech whose husband, Horatio, supplemented their income by his other jobs as joiner, wheelwright and undertaker. Their whitewashed thatched cottage with creepers growing up to the eaves and the neatly walled front garden combines with the other buildings to make a picturesque village scene. The tall elm tree is at the junction with Mill Hill Road and beyond that are the outbuildings to Rookery Farm (see previous page).

Irby's first grocery shop, owned by Mr A Constantine and known as the Irby Stores, is pictured on the right c1928. Two further shops were built adjoining and to the right of Irby Stores about 1930 and then a third one was added which was Cooper's Printers and Stationers. This later became the present Post Office. The post master in the 1920s of the thatched Post Office shown here was Mr E R Jones who had a shop in Greasby (see page 60). His daughter ran the post office and as an additional income, teas and refreshments were served in the garden.

The Prince of Wales Inn in Thingwall Road, Irby, is pictured in 1904. The inn is the left part of the recently white-washed building, the remainder comprising two cottages. Built about 1880, it was licensed as a beer-house, unlike the other hostelry in Irby, The Anchor, which was fully licensed. It was last run as a pub by the Peers family and closed about 1920. During the Second World War the building was used as the headquarters of the Home Guard. It was demolished in the 1950s. Today the site is used as a car park adjoining the present Post Office.

This peaceful scene of Irby was taken in 1917, looking along Thingwall Road into the village. The Prince of Wales Inn, pictured above, is the far part of the building on the right. As this was only licensed for beer, much of the passing trade went to The Anchor which held a full licence. So, to supplement their income from beer, they advertised good stabling and behind the horse and cart is a sign for teas. The village stores and Post Office is the whitewashed building to the right of the two farm lads with the bullock.

53

Mrs Ellis's Everleigh Preparatory School is pictured in the front garden of 4 Coombe Road in 1948. It closed in 1957. Back row: Margaret Atkinson, Robert Watkins, —, David Barber, —, Christine McCoy, —, Pat Bridson, Margaret Honey, Colin McAllister, John Coles, Robin Williams, Diane Pennington. Third row: June Wright, Margaret Carsley, —, Ann Butler, Margaret Cubbin, Russell Black, Bruce McAllister, Randal Grundy, Colin Rossall, David Roberts. Second row: Susan Watkins, Alison Barber, Suzanne Wadlow, David Constantine, Valerie Allen, Avril Crone, Jenny Constantine, Mrs Swan, Mrs Beetham, Mrs Ellis, Miss Macleod, Ruth Harris, —, Tommy Allen, Ronnie Wright, —. Front row: Keith Ratcliffe, Suzanne Hughes, —, Robert Beetham, Peter Butler, Sandra Easton, Alison Gifford, Rosemary Bolton, Heather Black, Ian Boumphrey.

The cottage on the left which advertises teas and minerals on its end wall faces Thingwall Corner. Barnston Road is ahead and left, Pensby Road is off to the right and Arrowe Park Road is behind. The cottage which was demolished between the wars stands by what is now the junction with Landican Road. The stone gateposts in the wall straight ahead mark the entrance to Thingwall Hall. Built in 1849 by Captain Lilly, it became part of The Royal Children's Hospital c1920. It was demolished in the mid 1950s and flats were erected here in 1962, with the stone gateposts standing either side of the Torrington Drive entrance.

Irby Hill Farm is pictured on the left in 1910. It was here, at the farmhouse of Mr & Mrs Cooke, that the first meeting of the Primitive Methodists in Irby was held in 1869. The numbers attending grew and in 1881 the tin chapel, pictured on the right, was built at a cost of £130. Frank Lester was an organist here prior to the First World War in which he was awarded a posthumous Victoria Cross. Due to an increase in the congregation, the tin chapel became too small and in 1936 the present Methodist church was built on the outskirts of Irby. The small vestry at the rear is all that remains of the tin chapel on the original site.

This scout camp is pictured c1912 next to the tin chapel seen above. Following the inaugural meeting of the scout movement at Birkenhead YMCA in 1908, the first official scout camp was held here at Irby Hill Farm. In the 1950s an American contacted Mr Duddleston, one of those present at Baden-Powell's inaugural meeting, and asked to be taken to the farm where the first camp fire had been lit. Standing at the spot he solemnly stated, 'From that camp fire has the light been carried to light all camp fires of the world'. It was his intention to erect a memorial but he was dissuaded from so doing.

This photograph was taken from Mill Hill Road in 1898 shortly before the mill at Irby was demolished. This was the second mill in the area, the original one which dated back to at least 1291, had stood on the south side of Hill Bark Road near the quarry. The mill pictured here was built between 1709 and 1725. It was a post mill erected on a brick base. The upper wooden construction was built around a strong wooden pivot and could be turned by a wooden lever to face the prevailing wind. It ceased to be a working mill about 1885. The outbuildings have since been demolished and the miller's cottage in the background is now a public house called The Mill (see below).

The miller's cottage on the left is also pictured above. It was purchased in 1919 by George and Bertha Lumsden who opened The Old Mill cafe here in 1924. This was referred to locally for many years as Lumsden's Cafe. Besides serving refreshments, dances were held here two or three times a week. In 1938 the brewers, Higsons, bought the cottage after which it was intermittently rented out by the brewery. It was due to the many delays in the granting of planning permission that the original cottage was saved when building work finally commenced in 1978. A new pub called The Mill opened here in 1980.

HILL BARK, FRANKBY

Hill Bark, pictured from the air, is not all it seems. For this Elizabethan-style mansion was built only one hundred years ago and then not on this site. Robert Hudson, the soap manufacturer, had this black and white, half-timbered, pseudo-Elizabethan manor house called Bidston Court built on an outcrop of Bidston Hill in 1891 at a cost of £150,000. Mr E B Royden, a Liverpool ship owner, purchased Bidston Court. and From 1929/31 he had the building dismantled and re-erected on the site of his wife's family home, Hillbark, in Frankby. Wirral UDC purchased it in 1961 and used it as a home for the elderly. The mansion is currently for sale.

FRANKBY HALL.   250

Frankby Hall, a castellated and turreted building, was erected in 1847 by Thomas Royden. In 1818 he founded the shipbuilders, Thomas Royden & Sons. The lodge, which was demolished a few years ago, stood by the entrance to the grounds at the junction of Hillbark Road and Frankby Road. In 1932 the 810 acres of land and buildings of the Frankby Hall Estate were put up for auction. The hall and grounds were withdrawn at £5,000 and the property was later purchased for £12,500 in May 1938 by Wallasey Corporation for use as a cemetery. Part of the hall was converted into two chapels which were opened in May 1940.

Frankby Post Office is pictured on Frankby Green in the 1890's. From the early years of this century until c1936, the Post Office moved to premises close by, which is now called The Old Post Office House. It then moved back to its original site where three years earlier the local sorting office was set up in an adjacent farm outbuilding. It was operated by Clyde Fairclough (who was post master for 40 years from c1913) and five assistants, until the office was moved to Salacre Lane in Upton c1938. The present single storey extension was built in 1938 and in April 1991 it became a Community Post Office. In 1974 Frankby Green was made a conservation area.

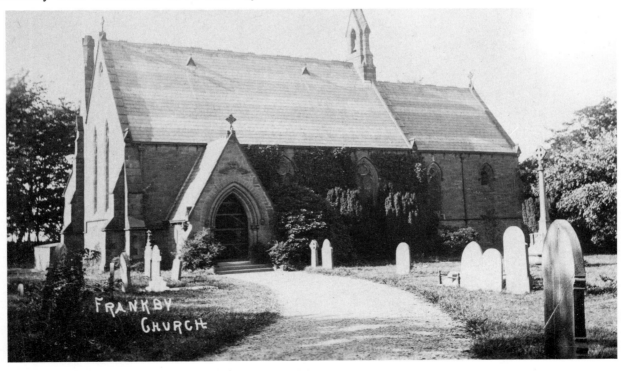

The parish of Frankby was created from the ancient parish of West Kirby in 1861. The new parish included the townships of Frankby and Greasby together with parts of the townships of Grange and Newton-cum-Larton. In April 1861 the foundation stone was laid and the church, which was dedicated to St John, was consecrated on 6 May 1862. The parsonage was also built at this time and survived until 1961 when, due mainly to dry rot, it was demolished. 147 Brookdale Avenue South had by then became the parsonage. In 1975 it was moved to its present address at 14 Arrowe Road.

Pump Lane, the road that connected Greasby with Meols, is seen here c1910. The lane received its name from the village pump which is set into the wall on the right. The trough can be seen in front of the boxed pump which would be filled with straw in the winter to protect it from frost. The pump was installed in the final quarter of the last century and was in use until some time after the First World War. As a result of the building of the Greasby by-pass, this part of the road fell into disuse, eventually becoming overgrown with brambles. In 1980 Jim O'Neil, a local historian, set up Operation Pump Lane which restored the pump.

This photograph was taken in Pump Lane c1928 when this was the main road between Greasby and Meols (see above). After the building of the Greasby by-pass in 1937/38, this part of Pump Lane was little used. Greasby Old Hall, built of red sandstone, dates back to the fifteenth century and its arched entrance with mullioned windows above is seen on the right. Inside was a large chimney-breast rising from the cellar through the ceiling; an attic room with oak beams and a large fireplace; and a priest's hole. During the Second World War this was the headquarters of the Auxiliary Fire Service.

The second Greasby Village Cross is pictured in Mill Lane. The original stone cross stood at the point of the triangular piece of land by the Coach & Horses Inn (see opposite) and this site has been suggested as the original village green. The stone cross was replaced by the pictured iron cross in 1862 by John Ralph Shaw, a landowner. He had the date and his own initials cast into the cross and it was placed in Cross Gardens (see picture below). In 1970 a plaque was placed at the base in memory of Councillor Pickerill.

Taken from Ashmount Farm in Greasby village (see opposite), this looks across to The Stores. From 1913 to 1931 these were owned by Mr E R Jones who lived with his wife and five children in Poplar House which is end-on and to the right of the shop. It was Mr Jones who published the E R J's Wirral Series of postcards during the period of the First World War, the photographer being Mr W S Foulger. The tree to the left is in Cross Gardens, which Mr Jones also owned. This is where the village cross stood for many years (see previous picture). Poplar House has been replaced by a bungalow but the shop is still in use.

This 1939 postcard was taken in Greasby Road looking toward the terraced cottages, known as Tea-pot Row, in the centre background. When this part of the road was widened in 1960, these cottages were demolished, as was the smithy opposite on the corner of Mill Lane in 1967. In its later years the smithy had diversified and was producing ornamental gates etc. The road on the left was blocked off at this junction and its only access was then from Mill Lane. The MG sports car on the left is in front of Hugh Rowe's saddler's shop and the Coach and Horses Inn. Ashmount Farm is behind the wall on the right (see picture below).

Ashmount Farm in Greasby village is shown behind the wall in 1910, with the picture opposite being taken from behind the gateway in the centre. This farmhouse almost certainly dates back to the eighteenth century. Being part of the Frankby Hall Estate, it was auctioned off in August 1932 when it was purchased by the then tenant, Mrs Griffith. The farm was auctioned again in 1977 and was granted a full liquor licence in June 1979. It then took two and a half years to renovate, opening as the Greave Dunning, a free house, in December 1981.

Annie Atkinson, the 1913 Greasby Rose Queen, is pictured with her attendants. The Greasby Fete was very popular but ceased with the outbreak of the First World War. In 1937 it was revived under the name of The Greasby & District Children's Sports and Fun Fair and was held in the field adjoining Frankby Church. In that year a team representing the Coach & Horses won the tug-of-war contest and the fair concluded with a fireworks display. It was intended to make this an annual event but war again intervened. It was revived for a short time after the Second World War when the procession ended in a field behind the Methodist Church.

Greasby village is seen here prior to 1910. The sign on the right reads:- 'Sydney R Fearnall, Auctioneer & Valuer, Chester. All classes of stock sold here every alternate Wednesday'. This was the site of Greasby's cattle market which now forms part of the car park for the Red Cat. This replaced the New Inn pictured centre, in 1962. Some one hundred years previously the New Inn was one of two licensed houses in Greasby. The building to the left of the inn is Manor Farm which has a 1680 date stone. Since 1972 it has been a restaurant and prior to that was a branch of the District Bank.

Looking along Arrowe Road into Greasby village c1930, Greasby Road is the main road ahead. Greasby Hall Farm and its outbuildings are seen on the left. In the 1930s MacDonald Drive was built to the left of the junction with Greasby Road, with shops beyond (see picture below). The New Inn (see previous picture) is in the centre background. The Library, Community Centre and Clinic have recently been built on land to the rear of the telegraph pole on the right.

This photograph of Greasby Road, c1955, was taken from the road junction pictured above. The shops were built in the mid 1930's to service the large number of houses being constructed. In 1935 four designs were advertised ranging in price from £490 to £600 or costing 12/=(60p) to 14/9(74p) per week. The latest type of wireless aerial was supplied with each house. The shops pictured here are from left to right :- Birkenhead Co-op; Wilkinson's, Ladies Outfitters; Alex Stewart, Wines and Spirits; Higginson's, Boot Repairers; Post Office; Frank Williams, Confectioners; Alan Dyson, Chemist; and Irwin's, grocers.

Greasby Road   Greasby   429

This photograph was taken in Greasby Road c1950. Wood Lane is on the left and a further block of shops was later built beyond the far ones. Land had been acquired near Rylands Hey where work on the building of a cinema was due to start in August 1936. However, this project never got off the ground. The entrance to Coronation Park, which opened in 1937, is by the car on the right. A small brick works which ceased production c1905 once stood on the site. The lay-by on the right was the course of the original main road which had been straightened when the by-pass was constructed 1937/38.

THE OLD ARROWE HILL

Taken in Arrowe Park Road, this photograph is looking along Arrowe Brook Road in the direction of Greasby in the 1920's. Arrowe House Farm on the right of some 150 acres was worked by Frank Burgess until the early 1940s. In July 1934 Sir Alan Cobham, with a team of twelve pilots, gave an aviation display on part of the farmland. He returned in May 1935 when flights cost from 4/ =(20p). Ken Adams farmed here for 25 years until 1966 when 39 acres of land was sold for light industry. Champion Sparking Plug Company now occupies this part of the site.